AF545233

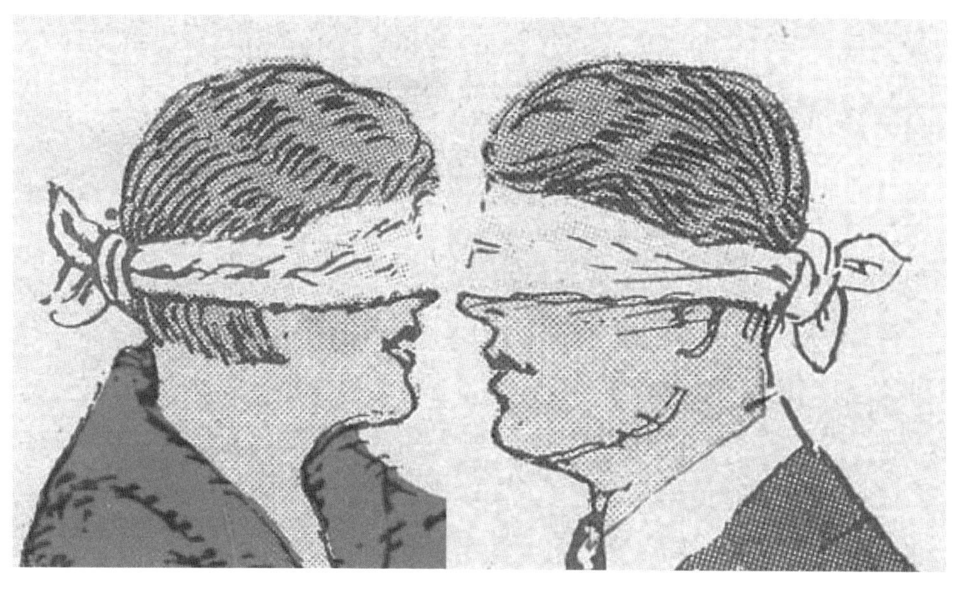

Love Emergencies

ALSO BY MAHMOOD KARIMI-HAKAK AND BILL WOLAK

Your Lover's Beloved: 51 Ghazals by Hafez (Cross-Cultural Communications, 2009)

ALSO BY BILL WOLAK

Poetry

Pale as an Explosion (The Somniloquist's Press, 1977)

Magazines Edited

Dream Helmet #1 (The Somniloquist's Press, 1977)

Free-For-All (The Somniloquist's Press, 1978)

ALSO BY MAHMOOD KARIMI-HAKAK

Poetry

Pebbles of Solitude

(Center for International Arts Press, 1992)

Rocks of Desire (MIA Press, Iran, 2003)

Translations into Persian

Roya-ye-Shab-e Nime-ye Tabestan / Shakespeare's *A Midsummer Night's Dream*

(Loh-e Simin Press, Iran, 1998)

Shive-ye Fanni-ye Namayeshnameh-Khani / David Ball's *Backwards and Forwards*

(Second edition, Loh-e Simin Press, Iran, 1998)

(First edition, Gol Press International, Iran, 1995)

Books Edited

Advanced Studies in Persian, Book III: *A Glance at Contemporary Persian Literature*

(The Academy of Language Press, Iran, 1975)

Advanced Studies in Persian, Book II: *Pre-Modern and Modern Persian Poetry*

(The Academy of Language Press, Iran, 1974)

Advanced Studies in Persian, Book I: *The Classics*

(The Academy of Language Press, Iran, 1974)

FORTHCOMING BY MAHMOOD KARIMI-HAKAK AND BILL WOLAK

Selected Poetry of Iraj Mirza

Iranian Love Amulets: The Folk Art of Seduction, Attraction, and Protection

Love Emergencies

Poems in English and Persian by

Bill Wolak

&

Mahmood Karimi-Hakak

Cross-Cultural Communications

Merrick, New York

2010

Published in the United States by
Cross-Cultural Communications
239 Wynsum Avenue, Merrick, NY 11566-4725/USA
Tel: (516) 868-5635
Fax: (516) 379-1901
E-mail: cccpoetry@aol.com
www.cross-culturalcommunications.com

Library of Congress Control Number: 2010934475
ISBN 978-0-89304-480-0
ISBN 978-0-89304-481-7 (pbk.)

Art on Front and Back Covers:
Erotic Flashcards #7: The Weight of a Blindfold, 2004, collage 7" × 9",
by Stefan Jamiolkowski

Photographs of Mahmood Karimi-Hakak and Bill Wolak: "Hafez Sounds Like Freedom" tour
Photograph of Bill Wolak by Mahmood Karimi-Hakak
Photograph of Mahmood Karimi-Hakak by Farah Taheri
Cover design by Steven Frim
Book design by Mahmood Karimi-Hakak and Bill Wolak
Page layout by Minoo Hosseini
Printed in the United States of America

For Maria

and

Baran & Shaparak

We must be the change we wish to see in the world.

–Mohandas Gandhi

Acknowledgments

Parts of the contents of this book have been published in magazines and in book form.

Bill Wolak's poems first appeared in the following magazines:
Pegasus Dreaming, Crack: A Journal of Poetry, The Art Factory, Beyond Doggerel, Over the Transom, Poetry Motel, Re: Verse!, Journal of New Jersey Poets, ZXY Magazine, and *Alpha Beat Soup*.
Mahmood Karimi-Hakak's poems first appeared in the following books: *Pebbles of Solitude* (Center for International Arts, Washington DC, 1991) and *Rocks of Desire* (MIA Press International, Tehran, Iran, 2001).

We would also like to acknowledge the following individuals who have read parts or all of the manuscript and provided us with generous feedback: Fariba Rofougaran, Pari Esfandiari, Naton Leslie, Maria Bennett, Philip Cioffari, Fatemeh Keshavarz, Ralph Blasting, Farzin Tafazoli, and Kayvan Asgari.

CONTENTS

PREFACE

The book of poetry you are about to read is a new experience in uniting two searching souls and merging together two passionate and intense lyrical languages. There is nothing new about inspiring one another or exchanging writings. Numerous poets have done so before. Sometimes poets have collaborated closely in translating one another's poetry by attempting to get to know each other's perspectives. The goal is always the same: reaching the inexpressible core of each other's thoughts. *Love Emergencies* has made use of these strategies, but it is fundamentally a different kind of work.

Bill Wolak and Mahmood Karimi-Hakak, after years of companionship and a deep understanding of each other's encounter with life, have decided to compose *Love Emergencies* as a concurrent journey undertaken by two seekers. At times, it feels as if they are walking side by side. But then it quickly turns into instances of chasing one another in a game of hide-and-seek. Soon after, they appear totally mesmerized by each other's pieces. And then there are those poems in which they each seem to feel completely on their own, a kind of solitary experience.

They each write their poems and at the same time echo the voice of the other through the medium of translation. Their profound familiarity with each other's thought processes and languages enables them to compensate for the limitations and hurdles created by moving from language to language. In many instances, their poetic companionship enables them to turn such hurdles into opportunities. An example of this is Hakak's fine piece:

Che khasteh bood khiyalam
as edaameh-ye shab
va entezaar-e toloo'
keh sobhdam be naveedee shegeft aaghaazeed.

In the English remaking of this poem, Bill translates the concept of being tired of *edaameh-ye shab*, which points to the lingering presence of the night, but is not necessarily devoid of hope, into "because of the interminable night." A reader, who follows both languages, will note that "interminable" introduces a hint of despair not present in the Persian poem. However, Bill is aware of that. He compensates almost immediately by translating the wondrous news of the arrival of the morning in "*naveedee shegeft sobh*" into: "When morning began with astonishing delight." The light emanating from a sense of delight wipes out any possible despair caused by the thought of the interminability of the night. Similarly, in Bill's "It's Dangerous Not to Love," the piece which is vital to the collection, Mahmood Karimi-Hakak transports some of Bill's finest poetic moments into their new linguistic habitat in Persian so naturally that the sense of translation disappears almost completely. Bill writes:

And you emerge from me
not as a photograph entrusting
its single memory to paper,
but as an ear's reminder
of what the eye can never reach.

The complicated concepts of emerging from someone other than oneself, or the transitory nature of a photograph on paper, are both very difficult to be recreated without too much loss in the new language. Mahmood gives us one of his most successful renderings here by making use of the concept of *tolooe'* [rising] to illustrate the emergence leading to a lasting presence:

Va to dar man toloo' meekonee
nah be-goone-ye aksee
keh yaadegaar-e lahzeh-ee khod ra beh kaghazee meeseparad

balkeh shaneedan-e aancheh ra
keh chashm nemeetavaanad deed.

Iranians and Americans know little about each other's poetic tradition. If we leave out a handful of well-known figures, such as Rumi, Emerson, Omar Khayyam, Steinbeck, and the like, the familiarity is almost zero. Before living in the United States, I had not heard of fabulous poets such as William Stafford, Billy Collins, Mary Oliver, Stanley Kunitz, and many others. I did not know that one of the finest gifts of America to the world is its poetry. In a similar way, most of my American friends are astounded at the quality of the poetry produced in contemporary Iran by poets, such as Forugh Farrokhzad, Sohrab Sepehri, and Ahmad Shamlu. For them, it is a delightful discovery that Persian poetic creativity did not come to an end after classical figures such as Hafez and Khayyam. It continues at a superb level to this day.

We live in dangerous times, fraught with social and political risks often deepened by our sense of loneliness and lack of trust in one another. The danger gets more formidable, and harder to understand, with cultural ignorance. In this chaotic environment, if there is any hope of reaching out to others, its key is human art and creativity. For this reason, the bridge that Bill Wolak and Mahmood Karimi-Hakak have built with their poetic moments to keep their worlds connected is to be cherished. It is a window that opens onto a new day.

Creating this collection is itself a poetic act. Its most memorable verse: "It's dangerous not to love."

–Fatemeh Keshavarz
Washington University, St. Louis
Summer, 2009

FOREWORD

Of Exigencies and Ecstasies

Paul Valéry declared, "Bodies born by chance can only be by chance harmonious." Although "born by chance" friendship never endures by happenstance. All associations are intrinsically alignments of shared interest and common cause. Those associations that flourish over time form a tribute to the energy and enthusiasm necessary to remain connected in a world overwhelmed with the unrelenting immediacy of interruptions, change, and distractions. For over thirty years, Mahmood Karimi-Hakak and Bill Wolak have sustained a friendship, although they have been separated geographically during most of that time. The two met at Rutgers University, where they were both graduate students, Mahmood in Theater Arts and Bill in Comparative Literature.

What made the present book possible is that over the thirty years that they have known each other, Mahmood and Bill have constantly shared their enthusiasms, worked on projects together, and supported each other's endeavors. During all that time, Bill has lived in New Jersey, while Mahmood has led a more peripatetic existence moving from New Jersey to New York, Belgium, Tehran, Maryland, and Texas. In all that time, they stayed in touch by mail, phone calls, and occasional meetings. Bill attended Mahmood's theater productions, documentaries, and independent films in New York and Maryland, and Mahmood attended Bill's poetry readings in New Jersey and New York City. In addition, they began to attend conferences together which concerned various aspects of the Middle East. About eight years ago, the two began talking about translating Hafez, but the project was put on hold while Mahmood worked for a year at Southern Methodist University in Dallas. Later, in 2002, when Mahmood accepted a position at Siena College in Albany, the Hafez project began. Translating Hafez developed into a way of integrating a deeper dimension into their friendship. Translating, in fact, became a long meditation on love, longing, loss, and liberty. The result was their book *Your Lover's Beloved: 51 Ghazals by Hafez* published by Cross-Cultural Communications in 2009. An additional consequence of their collaboration on the Hafez project was the decision of Bill Wolak to take a leave of absence from his teaching position to join a peace delegation to Iran in 2007, which was sponsored by the Fellowship of Reconciliation, one of America's largest and oldest interfaith peace and justice organizations. Coincidently, that trip included a visit to Shiraz, Hafez's hometown, and to his tomb as well.

Another difference between the two poets is the very real process of censorship which an Iranian poet must confront in order to be published in Iran. When Mahmood's book, *Rocks of Desire*, which he wrote in Persian in the 1990's while living in Iran, was published in Tehran, the manuscript had to be approved by the Ministry of Culture and Islamic Guidance before it could be printed. After publication, fifty copies had to be presented to the same ministry in order to obtain permission to release the book. In most cases, such a process has a chilling effect on the free expression of ideas. Any references to the political realities in Iran would be deleted. Take, for example, the following lines from "Your Midnight-Colored Hair":

The night hides itself
within the waves of your hair
so that deceitful ascetics
escape from the nightmares
    of lovers they've imprisoned,
and the dawn of recklessness
begins in the hands of youth
    who are always on call.

When the publisher submitted the following stanza to the censors, only the first two lines were acceptable; the rest were expurgated. Why the reference to "deceitful ascetics" would be considered anathema is clear. The reference to the "youth / who are always on call" is a more arcane allusion which refers to the *Basijis*, a self-appointed branch of the Revolutionary Guards between the ages of twelve and eighteen who are used to intimidate those who do not observe the strict Islamic dress code, as well as other malcontents and "enemies of the state."

In order to circumvent the censors, the publisher devised a trick in which two different editions of the book were actually printed, one with all the censor's deletions to be submitted to the ministry printed in larger type size in order to maintain the same number of pages as the actual book and another edition written in a smaller print size which maintained the entire text as he had written it. Publishing such poetry in Iran, needless to say, is a dangerous enterprise.

One common theme in both poets is the primacy of love in a world steeped in alienation, oppression, evanescence, and rapacity, hence the title of the book *Love Emergencies*. For Mahmood, love is clearly the central theme of his selections:

Let me breathe your beauty
so that I
inspired by you
can ignite these people
with love,
and these lovers
would radiate
your light
that shimmers like a silken camisole,
the prism of dusk,
or a forest at dawn ...

For Bill, too, the immediacy of love is central to his concept of praxis:

Claim the right to praise
returning even from what cannot be solved

or saved with abundance of kindness.
Risk everything
to offer, to strengthen,
to forgive.

Speak only to unite the one waiting
with the one who could wait no more,
to connect the loved one
with the one loving.

Mahmood's early influences include Sufism, Hafez, Rumi, and later the poetry of Forough Farrookhzad and Sohrab Sepehri. His poems are simultaneously intimate, political, and metaphysical. He frequently employs juxtaposition for emphasis, such as the following stanza concerning evanescence, where he contrasts the living embrace with the memory of the dead:

Kind one,
how startled I felt
to stare at those gravestones
while pressing you against my body
and to remember suddenly a destitute father
    who's sleeping calmly
    under mud-making rain
    that warms cold earth.

Bill, on the other hand, credits several contemporary poets for influencing him the most: Charles Henri Ford, Philip Lamantia, Michael McClure, Leonard Cohen, Kenneth Rexroth, and, of course, Allen Ginsberg. His poems reach into dreams and nightmares for much of their imagery:

Between the haphazard penetrations
of your presence and absence,
a door floats to the surface of the water.

On it we have fallen asleep entangled
and are adrift as if on an iceberg
with every hour a little less domain
and a little more of the sea.

The influence of Sufism and Surrealism is apparent in both of their respective works, and during the translation process what Mahmood has sufified in Bill, Bill has surrealized in Mahmood.

–Maria Bennett
Spring, 2009

INTRODUCTION

An Experiment in Translation

"The heart. The head. Switch them around."
The Third Master, *El Topo* by Alexandro Jodorowsky

Love Emergencies was conceived in 2005 during a harrowing car ride through tortuous traffic to LAX, following a Hafez reading that we gave in Los Angeles. At some point, Mahmood began reciting one of his poems in Persian from memory in response to an Iranian-American friend's question. Bill asked for a literal translation of the passage. Mahmood, in response, was hard-pressed to convey either the literal or political point of the passage in English. Out of that humble beginning developed the idea to produce a work which would attempt to translate Mahmood's work into English and Bill's into Persian.

The translation project would experiment with how Bill's poems would sound in Persian, and conversely, how Mahmood's poems would read in English. For the next three years, we met, discussed, and scrutinized each other's poetry, finally settling on the scheme of selecting ten representative poems to be presented bilingually. Translating each other's poems turned out to be a vastly different experience methodologically than working on Hafez. Instead of starting from an interpretation of an inscrutable text, each poet was able to explain precisely what was meant by an idiomatic phrase, a figure of speech, a problematic allusion, or a surprising juxtaposition. Despite the meticulous care in understanding the intention of the poet, there were places where meaning remained elusive. Unexpectedly, working on each other's poems was no less perplexing than translating Hafez. Each of the twenty poems selected went through five to ten different versions before a final text could be agreed upon.

Love Emergencies evolved as an experiment in translation in which we sought to communicate our most intimate thoughts and feelings across language and culture without footnotes. Such a project was, of course, a quixotic endeavor, since it obliged each poet to speak through the other's voice, sidestepping the inexorable contextual problems. In translations between related languages, for instance two Romance languages, the task is simplified by the existence of direct cognates, shared linguistic structure, and similar cultural assumptions. The further afield the two languages and cultures are, the more demanding the translator's work becomes. Words become enigmas, riddles, or puzzles. Meaning stretches and morphs from one language to another. The linguistic drawbacks become dizzying. Nevertheless, any translation is never expected to comprise the ultimate representation of the poem from one language to another. Rather, the translation serves as a means to encourage others to build upon the original foundation that the poet is offering. Perhaps the most appreciable difference between writing poetry in Persian and English is the irrepressibly oral nature of Persian poetry in general. In Persian, one "says" a poem; whereas, in English one "writes" a poem. Iranians incessantly recite or read poetry to each other. In English, poets are satisfied to publish a book that will be read by an audience. Only a specialized audience would ever hear the poem spoken by the poet or, for that matter, the poem read aloud.

The structure of the book requires some explanation. To begin with, since we always conceived of the book as being bilingual, various ways of organizing the translations and the original poems of each poet were possible. After experimenting with several more traditional formats, we settled on the present structure of the book, which offers a sense of otherness to both English and Persian readers because it must be read from two directions. From the English reader's orientation, the book begins with Bill's original poems on the left hand side and their Persian translations facing on the right hand side. Those reading the Persian translation must read following the orientation of the English, but since most of Bill's poems are one page, fewer complications arise. On the other hand, opening the book in the traditional Persian manner, all the individual parts of the book are repeated in Persian with Mahmood's poems presented first. Reading the English translations of any poem longer than one page from this side of the book, the English reader will be following the Persian orientation and experience reading the text "backwards." Thus, the English translation follows the lead of the Persian text and must be read in the opposite direction from the traditional order of the poem.

Translation, for us, became a means of breaking down cultural preconceptions, unexamined literary stereotypes, and stubborn prejudices. When examined in this manner, even simple words like wine or dance contained culturally specific associations for the West. For instance, some phrases like Bill's "dance floor to make time new" are almost impossible to translate into Persian because they foreground the culture's presuppositions; in this case, dancing violates the prevailing, intrusive prohibition against couples even touching in public; dancing by necessity, then, is relegated to private, autonomous spaces outside the regime's control, and, therefore, must convey a distinctly different denotation and connotation in Iran. On the other hand, most Persian allusions to legends, literature, and religion are lost on the average American reader. For instance, most Westerners would not know the legend of Arash that Mahmood alludes to in one of his poems. Arash, the hero who overcame humiliation for his country, was allowed to expand the size of the Persian kingdom as far as he could shoot an arrow; using his magic bow, he shot an arrow farther than anyone thought possible. Literary and religious allusions are even more problematic. Whereas some Westerners might recognize the word "Hadith" as a saying of the Prophet Muhammad, even few Persian speakers would recognize that Mahmood's lines "and your lips / –with such delicacy / that it completed my humanity– / sang a song of attraction" is alluding to the famous stanza from Ahmad Shamlu's poem "Aida in the Mirror" which reads in Ahmad Karimi-Hakak's translation as:

Your lips, delicate as poetry
turn the most voluptuous kiss
into such coyness
that the cave-animal uses it
to become human.

Although sealed in language on the page, these poems are seldom content to yield to their own limitations. Instead, they are always straining to reach beyond language into the turmoil of actual experience, where, as in a real emergency, when everything is at stake, language gets left behind and the body takes over –waving goodbye, touching a hand, opening into an embrace.

–Bill Wolak and Mahmood Karimi-Hakak
Spring, 2009

To Praise and to Forgive

Out of the rope's waiting embrace
and the knot's memory of darkness,
teach what it means to use hands.

Help to gather everything lost or useless
with words which will guard
what is most alive.

From the young gossiping
and the old remembering,
dare to hide nothing
till the young grow fond of remembering
and the old at last forget.

ستایش و بخشایش

از میان ریسمان انتظار هماغوشی
و خاطره‌ی تاریک گره
معنای استفاده از دست را بیاموزان.

کمک کن
تا هر آن‌چه را که بی‌تأثیر است و از دست‌رفته
با کلامی که پاسدار زنده‌ترین‌هاست
جمع‌آوری شود.

جرأت کن
تا چیزی از آن‌چه جوان به شایعه می‌سازد
یا پیر به خاطره می‌پردازد
پنهان نکنی
تا جوان به بلوغ خاطره‌پردازی برسد
و پیر به آرامگاه فراموشی.

١٠٥

Claim the right to praise
returning even from what cannot be solved
or saved with abundance of kindness.

Risk everything
to offer, to strengthen,
to forgive.

Speak only to unite the one waiting
with the one who could wait no more,
to connect the loved one
with the one loving.

طلب کن
حق ستایش بازگشت آن چیزی را
که حتی با انبوهی از مهربانی هم
نه حل‌شدنی‌ست و نه نجات‌یافتنی.

خطر کن همه را
دادن را
قدرت دادن را
بخشیدن را.

کلامی بگو که بپیوندد
او را که منتظر است
با او که دیگر انتظار نمی‌تواند
که بیامیزد
او را که دوست دارد
با او که دوستش می‌دارد.

It's Dangerous Not to Love

I describe you to explain myself;
you are the context for my possibilities;
so my words belong to you because in the end
it's dangerous not to love.
And you emerge from me
not as a photograph entrusting
its single memory to paper,
but as an ear's reminder
of what the eye can never reach.

Two directions; one crossroad.
I: a rainmaker conjugating absences.
You: a dance floor to make time new.
I always approaching you,
finding your nakedness everywhere,

دوست نداشتن خطرناک است

تو را توصیف می‌کنم
تا تعریف من باشی
تو زمینه‌ی امکانات منی
پس کلامم از آن توست
چرا که در پایان
دوست نداشتن خطرناک است.
و تو در من طلوع می‌کنی
نه به گونه‌ی عکسی
که یادگار لحظه‌ای خود را به کاغذی می‌سپارد
بلکه شنیدن آن‌چه را
که چشم نمی‌تواند دید.

دو راه؛ یک تقاطع
من باران‌سازی در شمارش غیبت‌ها
تو رقاص‌خانه‌ای نوساز فرصت‌ها.
من همیشه سراغ تو می‌آیم
عریانی تو را همه‌جا می‌یابم.

in the questioning spark of the blind man's eye,
in the sunlight warming gravestones,
in the embrace of an icebound harbor.
Always, I lick the thirst from your mirage.

Sometimes I disappear where you touch me;
sometimes the well of your body absorbs me
as I touch bottom.
Still, I explain you to describe myself.
You: the dream talking in many voices at once.
I: the sudden detachment of a wish expressed.

ــدر برق چشم جست‌وجوگر مردی کور
ــدر آفتاب گرمابخش بر سنگ‌قبرها
ــدر آغوش لنگرگاهی یخ‌بسته.
همیشه
زبان تشنه از سراب تو سیراب می‌کنم.

گاه
آن‌جا که مرا لمس می‌کنی
نابود می‌شوم
گاه که در خود رسوب می‌کنم
عمق وجود تو
فرو می‌کشد مرا.
و هنوز
من تو را توصیف می‌کنم
تا تعریف من باشی.
تو: رؤیایی که در آن چندین صدا
همزمان سخن می‌گویند
من: تفکیک ناگهانی آرزویی ابراز شده.

The Keeper of Strangeness

I am the light's fever in honey.
I am the lullaby heard in a nightmare.

In black-eyed alleys
and along tide calloused wharves,
I am the room where you find what you're missing.

I am the dial tone flesh of frightening energy transfers.
I am the expectant hands hovering over nakedness
and the insomnia of sperm.
My lap is a toolshed reaching dreamward.

I am the scarecrow made of birds.
I am the inexhaustible memory of salt.

Out of anger, I created the wind's solitude
Out of love, the restlessness of the rain's long inhalations.

I am the scream's only bridegroom.

پاسدار غربت

من تب نورم در عسل.
من طنین لالایی‌ام در کابوس.

من آن‌جایی هستم که تو گم‌کرده‌ی خود را می‌جویی،
در میان کوچه‌های کبود
در کناره‌ی پینه‌بسته‌ی بارانداز.

من ابراز آمادگیِ جسم‌ام
در لحظه‌ی تبادل نیروی ترسناک،
من دست انتظارم
بر فراز عریانی و بی‌قراریِ شهوت.
آغوش من خواستار رؤیایی‌ست ناآمده.

من مترسکی هستم ساخته از پرنده‌ها.
من خاطره‌ی خستگی‌ناپذیر عطشم.

من از خشم تنهایی باد را آفریدم،
از عشق بی‌قراریِ دم‌کشیده‌یِ باران را.

من داماد فریادم.

To Find the Position of the Heart

Give away your hands
to be able to hold.
Offer your dreams
to be safe from illusions.

Give up your voice
to be able to sing.
For a deeper silence,
surrender everything left unsaid.

Give out your tongue
to be able to thirst.
Offer what you possess
for what you can conceive.

Only what you have
yielded is yours.
From what you have given freely,
gather your heart.

یافتن جای قلب

دستت را هدیه کن
تا در آغوش بگیری.
رؤیایت را ببخش
تا از فریب در امان باشی.

صدایت را هدیه کن
تا خواندن بتوانی.
نگفته‌ها را رها کن
تا به عمق سکوت ره یابی.

زبانت را هدیه کن
تا به تشنگی برسی.
دارایی‌ات را ببخش
تا به ادراک برسی.

تنها آن‌چه هدیه کرده‌ای
از آن توست.
قلبت را در آن‌چه آزادانه هدیه کرده‌ای
بجوی.

37

Bruise

Echoing blueness,
color of the impossible darkness
inside bells.
Blue awakening sting
of an embrace which still makes
distance smile.

You have made yours
the riverbed of my flesh
where night always returns
to drink from your hands.

You have made yours
this living fingerprint
in which I feel you
holding me from within.

کبود

پژواک نیلگون
آن رنگ غیرممکن تاریکی
در اندرون کاسه‌ی ناقوس‌ها.
سوزش کبود بیداری
از هماغوشی‌ای که هنوز
لبخندی دور به لب می‌آرد.

تو کبودی خود را
جویبار پیکر من کرده‌ای
آن‌جا که شب همیشه تکرار می‌شود
تا از میان دست تو بنوشد.

تو کبودی خود را
این نقش زنده‌ی انگشت کرده‌ای
که در آن
حس می‌کنم تو مرا
از درون گرفته‌ای.

Song of the Door That Surfaced

Between the haphazard penetrations
of your presence and absence,
a door floats to the surface of the water.
On it we have fallen asleep entangled
and are adrift as if on an iceberg
with every hour a little less domain
and a little more of the sea.

Now as if we were ever nearer,
I'm holding you with the simple grace
of weightlessness.

No dream's triumph of memory
could surpass

آواز دری که به سطح نشست

در میان حلول گه‌گاهی
بود و نبود تو
دری
بر سطح آب شناور است.
بر آن، ما
پیچیده در آغوش هم
خوابیده‌ایم
چون بر کوه یخی غوطه‌ور
و آب هر لحظه گسترده‌تر می‌شود
و خاک
دورتر.

اکنون
گویی که هرگز این‌گونه نزدیک نبوده‌ایم،
من،
با شکوه ساده‌ی بی‌وزنی
تو را در بر گرفته‌ام.

هیچ رؤیای پیروزی خاطره‌ای نیست

the feeling of your flesh
vulnerable as the punched face of a sleeper.
No photograph's archeology of light could capture
all the possibilities of balance
you offer me.

With only a door between our embrace and the sea,
we are simply sleeping–
as if we were never farther apart,
as if we were holding each other
in orbit.

که حس جسم تو را
ـبه آسیب‌پذیری صورت له‌شده‌ی خفته‌ای ـ
برگذرد.

هیچ عکسی
با رسوب لایه‌های نور بر هم
نمی‌تواند
تمامی امکانات تعادلی را
که تو به من می‌دهی
تصویر کند.

تنها با دری
حائل میان هماغوشی ما و دریا
به‌سادگی خفته‌ایم
گویی هرگز چنین دور نبوده‌ایم
گویی در آغوش هم
فلک را می‌گردیم.

Silence Worthy of Disturbance

Against the night's teeth of mirrors
she is holding a match to the sky.
Her body is a warm staircase of blood
awash with the scent of sleeping apples.

Her freckles are leaves fallen in lake water,
her hair a color invented in dreams.
And she moves with all the elegance of sunlight.

Every day she will guide
my pursuit of the unknown, a pursuit
which rescues the real with the unexpected.

Her lips are ripe as lightning,
and between the beats of her pulse
there exists a silence worthy of disturbance.

سکوت سزاوار شکستن

در برابر دندان آیینه‌های شب
کبریتی بر آسمان افروخته.
اندامش پلکانی گرم از خون
لبریز از عطر سیب‌های خفته.

با گیسوانش به رنگی که تنها در خواب می‌آید
و گندمک‌های صورتش
ـ چون گل‌های نشسته بر آب ـ
به وقار آفتاب می‌خرامد.

او مرا هر روز
در پیگرد نشناخته‌ها ره می‌برد
پیگردی که واقعیت را
با آن‌چه انتظارش نمی‌رود
نجات می‌دهد.

لب‌های او همچون بلوغ آذرخش
و در میان ضربان نبض‌اش
سکوتی‌ست سزاوار شکستن.

٨٧

Inside her flesh, my body disappears
into a mysterious softness
the way footprints underwater are swallowed by the tide.
Inside her flesh, my body disappears
into a desire as ageless as summer.

اندام من میان پیکر او
گم می‌شود به نرمی مرموزی
چون رد پایی که در جزر و مد آب
بلعیده می‌شود.
اندام من میان پیکر او
در اشتیاق جاودانه‌ی تابستان
نابود می‌شود.

Song of the Inconsolable Survivor

Other lives passed through me so quickly!
Still jealous as recurrent nightmares, they're
wailing at the bloated darkness ahead.
Like a nimble moon's elastic cord of light,
how briefly they illuminated my obscure scars.
And their visits remind me
that you do not look long into a pistol shot,
that you do not wear your own blood like make-up.

Face calm as a map, I move tenuously
like the earth constantly settling in a cemetery.
Now entire days pass even quicker
than the snapping string of a burning piano.

آواز بازمانده‌ای تسلی‌ناپذیر

زندگی‌های دیگری به شتاب در من گذشته‌اند.
آن‌ها هنوز
حسود کابوس‌های تکراری
تاریکی ورم‌کرده‌ای را که در پیش است
سوگوارند.
آن‌ها
چون بند چابک نور ماه
چه کوتاه بر زخم‌های من تابیدند.
و دیدارشان یادآور این بود
که تو به تیر طپانچه خیره نمی‌شوی
که تو خون خود را سرخاب روی خود نمی‌کنی.

من
چون خاک گورستان که مدام فرو می‌نشیند
با چهره‌ای به سکون یک طرح
آرام پیش می‌روم.

اکنون
روزها سراسر
حتی سریع‌تر از پاره شدن تار سازی در آتش
می‌گذرند.

۸۳ 

Against all odds I have survived
even the harassments of memory.
I have fertilized myself with farewells,
dredging among unremitting screams
for my own voice.

For me, all light is haunted.

برعکس آن‌چه باید
من
حتی از آزار خاطره‌ها هم
نجات یافته‌ام.

من
با بدرودها
خود را بارور کرده‌ام
و صدایم را
در میان فریادهای مداوم
پرورده‌ام.

برای من
همه‌ی نورها
ارواح‌اند.

Deep into the Erasures of Night

Other hands will touch this warmth
where nothing is deeper than willing flesh.

Your kiss, open as water, dissolves into mine
and somehow secret maps
are exchanged in our nakedness.

Now loving makes a ladder
out of flesh and its scars,
and we climb deep into the erasures of night.

Other hands will touch this warmth
when before surrendering to sleep
a caress still stalks beyond exhaustion
the enticing pinks in which rain
sleeps after lovemaking.

در ژرفای پوشش شب

دست‌های دیگری این گرما را لمس می‌کنند
آن‌جا که ژرف‌تر از تنی تشنه هیچ نیست.

به صراحت آب بوسه‌های تو بر لب‌های من حل می‌شوند
و به گونه‌ای نامعلوم
خطوط طرحی محرمانه
در عریانی ما مبادله می‌شوند.

اکنون معاشقه نردبانی می‌سازد
از جسم و جراحت
و ما به ژرفای پوشش شب
صعود می‌کنیم.

پیش از آن‌که خود را به خواب بسپاریم
وقتی ورای خستگی، هنوز
آن صورتی فریبنده
ـ که بعد از معاشقه‌باران در آن به خواب می‌رود ـ
نوازشی را منتظر است،
دست‌های دیگری این گرما را لمس می‌کنند.

Hands

Constantly reaching outward,
a hand is a caress at your disposal.
At the moment of departure,
hands are like mist evaporating in the sun.
At the moment of return,
they're like rabbits watching headlights
along the highway.
Dawn-eyed fingernails, naked as rope,
are the mirrors behind a hand's fingerprints.
Hands tracing the arch of a thigh
or celebrating a breast
are straining to enter flesh deeper than light;
they desire most the parts of a body
that only blood can reach.

دست

همواره باز رو به برون، دست
گویی نوازشی‌ست که در اختیار توست.
آن دم که می‌روی، مانند مه در آفتاب
نابود می‌شود.
و آن دم که باز می‌آیی
خرگوشی است، دست
ـمانده کنار راه خیره به نور چراغ‌هاـ
در انتظار تو.
و ناخن سپیده‌ی تابان، عریان چنان طناب
آینه‌ای‌ست در پس انگشت.
و دست
با لمس طاقی ران
یا در سرور صعود به پستان
ـپُر زورتر ز نورـ
تا بطن جسم عمیقات ره باز می‌کند.
تنها به جستجوی گوشه‌ای از تن
این دست می‌رود
که فقط خون
ره یافته در آن.

Bill Wolak is a poet whose work has appeared in many literary magazines and who has published one collection of poetry, *Pale as an Explosion*. His forthcoming book of poetry is entitled *Archeology of Light*. He has translated Joyce Mansour, Stuart Merrill, and Francis Vielé-Griffin. With Mahmood Karimi-Hakak, he has translated *Your Lover's Beloved: 51 Ghazals of Hafez*. Mr. Wolak has traveled throughout Asia, including trips to Tibet, Nepal, Thailand, Japan, and China. He has been awarded several National Endowment for the Humanities scholarships and two Fulbright-Hays awards to study and travel in India. In the Spring of 2007, he was selected to participate in a Friendship Delegation to Iran sponsored by the Fellowship of Reconciliation, the nation's largest and oldest interfaith peace and justice organization. Mr. Wolak has been an Adjunct Professor in the English Department at William Paterson University for over twenty years.
williamwolak@netzero.net

بیل والک شاعری است که شعرهایش در بسیاری مجله‌های ادبی و یک دفتر شعر به نام **به بیرنگی یک انفجار** به چاپ رسیده است. کتاب تازه‌ی او *Archeology of Light* نام دارد. او Stuart Merrill، Joyce Mansour و Francis Vielé-Griffin را به انگلیسی ترجمه کرده است. **معشوق عشق تو: ۵۱ غزل از حافظ**، اولین کار مشترک او و محمود کریمی حکاک است که در سال ۲۰۰۹ توسط Cross-Cultural Communications منتشر شد. بیل والک تاکنون به چند کشور آسیایی از جمله تبت، نپال، تایلند، ژاپن و چین سفر کرده و برای سفر به هندوستان و تحقیق درباره‌ی شعر آن کشور به دریافت چندین بورس و National Endowment for the Humanities دو جایزه‌ی Fulbright-Hays نائل شده است. وی در سال ۲۰۰۷ از طرف یکی از Fellowship Of Reconciliation قدیمی‌ترین و بزرگ‌ترین سازمان‌های صلح و دوستی برای شرکت در یک Friendship Delegation انتخاب و به ایران سفر کرد. پروفسور والک حدود بیست سال است که به عنوان استاد پاره‌وقت در دانشگاه ایالات William Paterson نیو جرسی ادبیات انگلیسی تدریس می‌کند.

Mahmood Karimi-Hakak, Artistic Director of Mahak International Inc., is a poet, writer, translator, theater director, and filmmaker. His literary credits include five plays, two books of poetry, several translations, and numerous articles and interviews both in English and Persian. He has produced, created, choreographed, directed, designed, and acted in over 50 stage plays, dance performances, and films. Mahmood's artistic works have participated in national and international film and theatre festivals in America, Europe, and his native Iran, and have gained him three awards: Best Director (1979), Outstanding Foreign Film (1995), and Critics' Choice (1999). His academic achievements include a Raymond C. Kennedy Award (2005) and a Fulbright (2009). Professor Karimi-Hakak has taught at CUNY, Towson, and Southern Methodist universities in America as well as universities in Belgium and Iran. At present, he serves as Professor of Creative Arts at Siena College in New York. mhakak@siena.edu

محمود کریمی حکاک، مدیر گروه هنرمندان بین‌المللی محک، شاعر، نویسنده، مترجم، کارگردان تئاتر، و فیلم‌ساز است. کارهای ادبی او شامل پنج نمایشنامه، دو دفتر شعر، چند ترجمه‌ی کتاب و تعدادی نقد، مصاحبه و مقاله به فارسی و انگلیسی می‌باشند. کریمی حکاک در بیش از پنجاه نمایش، رقص و فیلم به عنوان کارگردان، تهیه‌کننده، بازیگر، طراح و نویسنده شرکت داشته که بسیاری از این آثار در جشنواره‌های بین‌المللی چون ادینبارو، آوینیون و نیویورک ارائه شده و برای او سه جایزه‌ی هنری به ارمغان آورده‌اند: کارگردان ممتاز برای نمایش ***شور عاشورا***، ۱۹۷۸؛ فیلم برجسته‌ی خارجی برای فیلم ***درد مشترک***، ۱۹۹۵ و جایزه‌ی هیئت منتقدان برای نمایش ***رؤیای شب نیمه‌ی تابستان***، ۱۹۹۹. وی هم‌چنین در سال ۲۰۰۵ به اخذ جایزه‌ی تحقیقاتی Raymond C. Kennedy و در سال ۲۰۰۹ به دریافت بورسیه‌ی Fulbright نایل شده است. پروفسور کریمی حکاک در دانشگاه‌های Towson، Southern Methodist و دانشگاه شهری نیویورک در آمریکا و دانشگاه‌های بلژیک و ایران تدریس کرده و هم‌اکنون با سمت استاد هنرهای خلاق و مدیر گروه تئاتر در دانشگاه Siena در ایالت نیویورک به تدریس مشغول است.

Her vast and generous lap
was a resplendent meadow
full of colors,
scents,
and secrets.

And that time
my hands,
frail, delicate,
picking flowers and playing songs, free
singing and dancing,
in the vast meadows of your bleeding lap,
seized the base anger
of that petrified, old man
with the new blossoming buds
of law.

And they rescued the night,
which had wandered through the city
with its bat-like shape,
from darkness and despair.

❊ ❊ ❊

The frail and delicate hands
–patient and tender–
saved us from being ambushed
by hatred
and
revenge.

دشتی شگرف بود
پر از رنگ و
بوی و
راز
دامان مهربان و وسیع او.

و آن زمان
دستی ظریف و پاک
گلچین و شعرخوان
ـآزادهـ
در ژرف دشت دامن خونین‌اش
رقصان و شادمان
خشم حقیر پیر تحجر را
در غنچه‌های نوشکفته‌ی قانون
اسیر کرد.

و شب را
که در عرض و طول شهر
با قامت خمیده‌ی خفاش‌گونه‌اش
به گردش نشسته بود
از تیرگی و غصه رهانید.

❊ ❊ ❊

دست ظریف
نرم و
صبور و
پاک
ما را نجات داد
از دستبرد انتقام و
تنفر.

That night
because of your dogmatic command
the candles imprisoned
in the cold morgue of your blind wisdom
were extinguished
            and buried.

That night
my body was broken,
        bloodied,
                bound,
                        and forgotten
by the enraged hands of an old man,
–the hands that had come to free us all–
in the torture chamber of Hadith
that was made of lies.

❊ ❊ ❊

Yes,
such was that day's decree!

What haven't they done to us?
What haven't I shared with you?
Until the time when the secret
of the door's lock was discovered,
and it opened,
and the inconsolable mother
disheveled and haggard
                wept blood.

آن شب
ولرم شمع تقارن
تنها
در سردخانه‌ی حکمت کورت
راهی گور گشت
و خاموشید.

آن‌شب
جسم مرا
خشونت دستی پیر
ـدستی که دست‌گیر رهایی باید می‌بودـ
در چنبر حدیث دروغش
بست و
شکست و
فراموشید.

* * *

آری
پیام روز چنین بود!

با ما چه‌ها که نکردند.
با تو چه‌ها که نگفتم.
تا آن زمان که رمز جادویی در
بشکست و باز شد
و مادر بی‌تاب
آشفته و متلاطم
گریست خون!

Not Much Time
Till Dawn for Dreaming

My patient lover announced night's message
with its arching, bat-winged shape,
"Not much time till dawn for dreaming."

❊ ❊ ❊

Was that your final verdict,
you who are drunk with the wine of hate?

Was saving that new-gained innocence
only possible because
of your hypocritical piety,
you whose ideology preaches
only in one direction?

❊ ❊ ❊

تا صبحدم
خیال درازی نیست!

شب را پیام داد
یار صبور من
در انحنای قامت خفاش‌گونه‌اش:
«تا صبحدم،
خیال درازی نیست!»

* * *

آیا
کلام آخر تو این بود
ای مست از شراب تنفر؟

آیا
نجات این نجابت نو پا
تنها به زهد شرمناک تو ممکن بود
ای عارض طریقت یک‌سویه؟

* * *

Fountains

How alone
I feel
tonight
wandering into
the city's delirium.

How bitter the confrontation
awaiting me
back home.

How the pounding
of my heart
echoes
your voice.

How far
I am
from holding
you.

❋ ❋ ❋

And fountains illuminated
the ecstasy of lovers at night.

و فواره‌ها...

چه
تنها
رها می‌شوم
در جنون شب شهر.

چه
بیداری تلخی
در خانه
در انتظارم نشسته است.

چه
قلبم
صدای تو را
می‌طپد باز.

چه
از بودن
با تو
دورم.

* * *

و فواره‌ها رنگ عشاق شب را کشیدند...

And the moon
(the lover and enchanter)
peered through the window
and with all the city's inhabitants
wailed
grieving your absence.

❊ ❊ ❊

Perhaps
dreaming you was enough
to reconcile me
once again
amidst poetry, flowers, and nightingales
with the depths
of my childhood's alleyways.

و ماه
عاشق و افسونگر
سر از میان پنجره بیرون کرد
و با تمام مردم شهر
از دست دوری تو
نالید.

* * *

شاید
خیال تو کافی‌ست
تا باز
در میان شعر و گل و بلبل
با عمق کوچه‌های کودکی‌ام
آشتی کنم.

you repeating poetry
through a canary's tiny throat,
and the reverberation of your voice
became the night's echoing undertow
within the day's sleeping sky,
and the pulse of the city was
in the process of remaking history
(that meaningless repetition of destruction).

And dreaming
–perhaps–
that the moon lingered facing you
and steeped the twirling of your dazzling curls
with my love's subtle perfume.

And dreaming
–perhaps–
that the moon
(messenger and message of praise)
arrived ecstatically to welcome you
and in every key
sang the song of love
to your appreciative ear.

And dreaming
–perhaps–
that your small hands
disappeared into my face.

که شعر می‌خواندی
تو
از میان حنجره‌ی کوچک قناری‌ها
و بازتاب صدایت
طنین جاری شب بود
در آسمان خفته‌ی روز
و نبض اجتماعی شهر
در دست بازسازی تاریخ
ـتکرار بی‌دلیل شکستن‌ها ـ

و خواب دیدم
ـشاید ـ
که ماه روبه‌روی تو بنشست
و در شکن‌شکن گیسوان طنازت
عطر لطیف عشق مرا پاشاند.

و خواب دیدم
ـشاید ـ
که ماه
(پیغمبر پیام ستایش)
رقصان به پیشباز تو آمد
و پرده پرده موسیقی عشق
در گوش مهربان تو خواند.

و خواب دیدم
ـشاید ـ
که دست کوچک تو
میان چهره‌ی من گم شد،

collapses into the mirror of love.
And the predestined moment
and blood
 and joy
 and freedom.

❊ ❊ ❊

I returned to myself
and the city
 and newness
 and light.

The blazing cherry blossoms,
the ambiguous trajectories of my wandering thoughts,
the gaze of an old man with infinite expectations,
and the ecstatic downbeat of the tambourine.
And I
in the middle of endless pouring rain
was wandering toward your hand,
and in the imagination of my dream-child,
I lifted you
above the cloud-covered mountains of tomorrow.

❊ ❊ ❊

How easily I slept within your gaze
dreaming
 –perhaps–

در انعکاس آینه‌ی عشق
و لحظه‌ی موعود
و خون
و لذت
و آزادی.

* * *

به خویش برگشتم
و شهر
و تازگی
و نور.

شکوفه‌های ملتهب گیلاس
خطوط مبهم اندیشه‌های سرگردان
نگاه پرتوقع مردی پیر
و ضرب شادی دف
و من
که از میان ریزش جاویدان
به‌سوی دست تو می‌رفتم
و در خیال کودک رؤیا
تو را
به قله‌های مه‌گرفته‌ی فردا
صعود می‌دادم.

* * *

چه ساده در نگاه تو خوابیدم
و خواب دیدم
ـشایدـ

Dreaming at Dawn Is Always Welcome

At dawn
amid my memories
you stretched your wings
and the journey began,
a journey into your innocent embrace.

❊ ❊ ❊

My hands and lips glide across your trembling flesh,
you gaze anxiously
at my enticing body,
and desire's stairway
leads to eternity.
And hundreds of bells begin clanging,
and thousands of fearless dervishes chant in unison
soaring beyond impossible heights,
and the ancient fortress of damnation

خواب سحر خوش‌ست
همیشه!

سحر
میان خاطره‌هایم
تو بال گستردی
سفر بیآغازید
سفر به پاکی آغوشت

* * *

تماس دست و لبم
با لطیف اندامت
نگاه مضطرب تو
به جسم مسحورم
و پله‌های خیال
کشیده تا ابدیت
و زنگ صد ناقوس
و های‌هوی هزاران قلندر بی‌باک
و پر کشیدن تا قله‌های ناممکن
و انهدام بناهای کهنه‌ی تکفیر

It was the occurrence of a new experience
that I,
        assured and determined,
with the unexpected stubbornness
of a child stealing pistachios,
                                        penetrated you.

And the night
arrived
dazzling with such splendors.

It was the occurrence of a new experience
which lifted us
beyond the best
of memories.

ظهور تجربه‌ای نو بود
که من
ـمصمم و بی‌باکـ
با لجاجت ناباورانه‌ی طفلی
که پسته می‌دزدد
تو را شکافتم.

و شب
به شکوهی شگرف
آغازید.

ظهور تجربه‌ای نو بود
که ما را
به اوج خاطره
پیوست.

and your look
–subtle
searching
seductive–
and the window's curious eyes,
and your warning,
"Shouldn't we draw the curtains?"
and my burning kisses,
and the paleness of your breasts,
and a mother's innocent sleep,
and the door
that wouldn't lock.
And I
exploring your body
with trembling heart and hands,
and the curling ivy of your hair
twined around the sturdy tree of my neck.
And the pounding of your anxious heart
with the first thrust
of my fearless flesh,
and the slight shivering of your body,
and the frightened feeling of guilt
and pain
and pleasure
and panic.

و نگاهت
ـظریف و
جست‌و‌جوگر و
شیطان ـ
و چشم کنجکاو پنجره
و کلامت
که
«پرده را بکشیم!»
و بوسه‌های ملتهب من
و سپیدی سینه‌ی تو
و خواب ساده‌ی مادر
و در
که قفل نمی‌شد
و من
که
لرزه‌ی دل و دستم
تو را وجین می‌کرد
و ناز پیچک مویت
که بر درخت تنومند گردنم پیچید
و تیک‌ـتاک مضطرب قلبت
در لحظه‌ی حضور جسم جسور من
و لرزش خفیفت وجودت
و حس خشمگین گناه
و
درد و
لذت و
ترس.

How Tired My Thoughts Were Because of the Interminable Night When the Morning Began with Astonishing Delight

Your eager glance
washed my tired body,
and at the height of the afternoon's silence
my voice dangled from your hair,
while
        drop
            by
                drop
my poem
        –praising your shoulders,
                and admiring your legs–
poured into your flawless lap.

Your hands caressing me
                                        began
the occurrence of a new experience
                                    out of persistent habits,

چه خسته بود خیالم
از ادامه‌ی شب
و انتظار طلوع
که صبحدم به نویدی شگفت آغازید

نگاه مشتاقت
وجود خسته‌ی من را شست
و در سکوت بالغ بعد از ظهر
صدای من به موی تو آویخت
و قطره
قطره
شعرم را
ـکه از ستایش شانه‌هایت
تا نیایش پایت
ادامه داشتـ
به عمق دامن باکره‌ات ریخت.

ظهور تجربه‌ای نو بود
در امتداد جاودانه‌ی عادت
که لمس دست تو باعث شد.

Poetry cascaded from
your lips like dew
dripping
from a
blossom.
And I
stared at you
astounded.

Your gaze
triggered an unending exchange of piercing
between us,
and inside my chest throbbed
a delirious thought.

❊ ❊ ❊

You
stayed patiently
still,
and the passing afterimage
dangled me
from memory.

شبنم شعر
از شکوفه‌ی دهانت
قطره
قطره
چکید،
و من
به تو
ـ سرگشته ـ
خیره ماندم.

نگاهت
نفوذی بی‌پایان را
در کنکاشی متقابل
باعث شد،
و خیال سر کنده‌ای
در سینه‌ام
طپید.

* * *

تو
با تأملی صبورانه
ماندی
و مرا
تصوری گذرا
از فراز خاطره
آویخت.

I Glimpsed a Prophecy in Your Curious Eyes

Your gaze
in search of a new Hadith
roamed over my drunken being,
and the clusters of your shyness
took refuge
in your blushing cheeks.

The waterfall of your night-colored hair
polished the span of your glistening shoulders,
and your lips
    –with such delicacy
        that it completed my humanity–
sang a song of attraction.

الهام واژه را
در چشم کنجکاو تو
دیدم

نگاه تو
در جست‌وجوی حدیثی نو
بلندای سرخوش وجود مرا گشت،
و گونه‌های منقلب‌ات
خوشه‌های شرم را
پناه داد.

آبشار شبرنگ گیسوی تو
پهنای بلور شانه‌ات را
صیقل داد،
و لبانت
به ظرافتی که تکامل انسانی مرا
رقم می‌زد
آواز آشنایی
سر داد.

for that temple of lies and deceit.

Every moment
with a hundred words of delight and desire
my hands
my lips
all my body
mingles with
the fire blazing
from inside you.

❊ ❊ ❊

Then
when in my mind
with the full weight of memory
I imagined you
as the most adored idol,
I laugh enigmatically
at my own thoughts.

آن معبد دروغ و ریا را)
سرد
توصیف می‌کند.

هر لحظه باز
با صد کلام شوق و تمنا
دستم،
لبم،
تمام تنم،
آغشته می‌شود
با آتشی تنوره‌کشان
از درون تو.

❊ ❊ ❊

آن‌گاه،
وقتی که در خیال خود
از تو
شاهین بتی به اعتبار خاطره‌ها ساختم عظیم،
بس عارفانه
به افکار خویش
می‌خندم.

My thoughts
amidst the hectic, crazy streets
–solitary,
broken,
tired,
and withdrawing–
remind me of you,
and then a thousand times
my hands that arouse fantasies
draw the noon's maturity
out of the delicate lines
of your determined face and body.

Your petite body
floating on the waves of my thoughts
becomes a tower
that I worship out of revenge.

And your curved, scratched cheeks
define my storm of kisses
amid passion and joy and damnation
at times
hot
as the passionate worship
of an old Magus keeping that fire alive,
at times
cold
as a condemned man's praise

فکر مرا
در شور و شر خیابان
تنها،
شکسته،
خسته،
گریزان
تو
یاد می‌کنی.
و
آن‌گه هزار بار
دست خیال‌پرور من
در نازکای چهره و اندام قاطعت
ظهر بلوغ را
تصویر می‌کند.

کوتاه قامت‌ات
در پستی و بلندی افکار نو رسم
به برجی
ـ که انتقام انگیزه ستایش آن است ـ
تعبیر می‌شود.

و گونه‌های مورب مخدوش‌ات
رگبار بوسه‌های مرا
در التهاب لذت و لعنت
ـ گه
(چون نیایش امشاسپند پیر
آن ایزد همیشه شعله‌وران را)
گرم
ـ گه
(چون ستایش محکوم معترف

My Own Thoughts
Are Mocking Me

My thoughts undulate
with provocations,
passions,
and feelings of guilt,
like the restless caterpillars
of your short, curling hair,
–undulations joyous as the ocean,
–undulations polished as the desert,
–and undulations trusting as a house's solitude,
and your moaning and murmuring
(the link between middle-age
and
desire).

My thoughts
open the door
of your delicate soul
into an ever-blossoming spring.

افکار من
مرا به سخره می‌آراید

فکر مرا،
میان حادثه و
شور و
حس گناه،
هزار پای بی‌قرار موی کوته تو
موج می‌زند
ـموجی به شادمانی دریا
ـموجی به انسجام کویر
ـموجی به اعتبار خلوت خانه
و آه و ناله تو
(پیوند مستقیم میان‌سالگی
و
تمنا.)

فکر مرا
روح ظریف تو
در باز می‌کند
سوی بهار همیشه مشجر.

What unkind impulse forces you
to become an obstacle
to a song's fleeting melody
–heartwarming
brief
and peaceful–
the song of a simple admirer
who prepares me
for you?

When a world full of desire
tries to climb up
your strong, muscular legs
in order to reach
the source of life inside you,
and mockingly you destroy
the dreams of future men,
your midnight-colored hair
pours down your arching back
to complete what's missing in mankind:
a path to dawn's appearance
and night's vastness
and tomorrow's purity.

کدام انگیزه‌ی تو را
آن‌چنان به تحرک وامی‌دارد
که ترنم آوازی را
ــدلگرم و
کوچک و
آرامــ
از معشوقی ساده‌دل
که مرا برای تو می‌آراید
مانع می‌شوی؟

آن زمان
که جهانی از تمنا
دو پای استوار تو را
می‌پیماید
تا به انسجام حیات
صعود کند،
و تو
اندیشه مردان آینده را
به تمسخر
ویران می‌کنی،
شبرنگ گیسوانت
هم‌چنان بر بلندای قامت‌ات
قد راست می‌کند
تا تکامل عریانی انسان را
راهی باشد
به طلوع غروب
به نهایت شب،
به گسترش روز
و نجابت فردا.

so that deceitful ascetics
escape from the nightmares
        of lovers they've imprisoned,
and the dawn of recklessness
begins in the hands of youth
        who are always on call.

The skillful painter,
searching for an astonishing myth
in which a man-god
    is shackled by chains,
uses the thickness of your hair
to silhouette the pale firmness of your chest
and to protect your breasts
        (those two drunken volcanos
            with rebellious elixir
                hidden within them)
from the feeble evil-eye
of the revenge-seeking, jealous lover.

What keeps your eyes so myopic
that they refuse
a refuge
        to a refugee
or a heart
    to a heartkeeper?

تا زاهدان ریاکار
در آستانه‌ی رؤیای عاشقان زندانی
بیاسایند
و طلوع جسارت
در کف نوباوگان همیشه در صحنه
بیاغازد.

نقاش چیره‌دست
از انبوه گیسوان تو سود می‌جوید
تا به جست‌وجوی اسطوره‌ای شگرف،
که در آن
انسان-خدایی را
به اسارت کشیده‌اند،
ستبر سپید سینه‌ی تو را
تصویر کند.
و دو پستانت را
(آن دو آتشفشان مست
که اکسیر جاودانه‌ی سرکش را
در بست
نهان کرده‌اند)
پوششی باشد
از چشم زخم عاجزانه معشوق کینه‌خواه.

کجای چشم تو این‌گونه کوچک است
که پناهی را
از پناه‌خواهی
دریغ می‌داری
و دلی را
از دلداری؟

Your Midnight-Colored Hair

You have spread your hair
as the prelude to a message
which invites the wandering
men of history
        from the other side of time
                to this side of desire.

Your hair glistens
like the full moon
radiating a light
in which other women brood
        over their uncertain, intermittent lovemaking,
as the ocean's thighs
        spread across the sky's vastness.

The night hides itself
within the waves of your hair

گیسوان تو شب بود

گیسوانت را
فراخوان پیامی گسترده‌ای
که مردان سرگردان تاریخ را
از فراسوی زمان
تا فراروی اندیشه
می‌خواند.

گیسوانت
شبرنگ ماهتابی است
که در تلألؤ آن
دیگر زنان
به همآغوشی مشکوک ماهیانه
می‌اندیشند
و اندام دریا
تا پهنای آسمان
کشاله می‌کند.

شب در امواج گیسوان تو
پنهان می‌شود

Begging from Here to an Acacia Tree Is a Dangerous Path

Stand up.
We must welcome the one arriving.
We must hurry
        to show our admiration.
We must worship
            the ultimatum
                of the acacia's perfume.

We must free ourselves
            from the present
                    by the power of memory.

❊ ❊ ❊

Certainly,
the sultan of love
was a worried ruler.

تا دست‌بوس اقاقی
چه راه پر خطری است

برخیز
باید به بدرقه رفت.
باید
به دست‌بوس شتافت.
باید
به حکم عطر اقاقی
نماز برد.
باید
ــبه زور خاطرهــ
از حال
دل برید.

* * *

آری
سلطان عشق
فرمانروای مضطربی بود!

Kind one,
your song's passionate melody
merged with my ecstatic dance
in the flickering candlelight.

Kind one,
how boldly you wrote,
"Plenty of pleasure will fill our visits,
and plenty of pleasure will fill our talks."

Kind one,
water out of water
air out of wind
leaf out of branch
–like you–
everything's vibrating.

Through the night
of your hair,
offer me the water's transparency,
time's movement,
and the rain's embrace.

نازنینا،
در سماع شمع
شور دم آواز تو
آن شب
با سرور وجد من
آمیخت.

نازنینا،
خوش نوشتی
بس
«لذت دیدار بسیار است
لذت گفتار هم بسیار.»

نازنینا،
آب از آب و
هوا از باد و
برگ از شاخ
می‌لرزند.

تو
میان گیسوی «شبدر»
آب را از آب و
زمان از حرکت و
آغوش از باران
فراوان کن!

who's sleeping calmly
under mud-making rain
that warms cold earth.

Kind one,
water out of water
earth out of earth
and dreaming out of awakening
became visible.
Night after night,
waiting for warmth of your kisses
(whose sounds I could hear
through the incessant telephone)
I savored our happy moments
till dawn.

Kind one,
uncontrollable love
streams out from your fingertips across the frets
of your setar
and creates a sleek sculpture of song,
and your voice
filled with delight and attentiveness
reverberates
through the empty room illuminated by moonlight.

ــآن خوب خفته
زیرگل باران زمین سرد.

نازنینا،
آب از آب و
زمین از اندرون و
خواب از بیدار
پیدا بود.

شب به شب
در انتظار بوسه‌هایت گرم
(که صداشان از درون گوشی پرحرف می‌آمد)
تا سپیده
می‌شمردم لحظه‌ها را
شاد.

نازنینا،
عشق
سرکش
می‌خرامید از نوک انگشت‌های تو
روی پرده‌های سازت
خوش‌تراش آواز
و صدایت
از غرور و مهربانی
پر
در فضای پاک پرمهتاب
می‌پیچید.

Kind One,
The Music of Your Instrument
Plants a Memory Deep in
My Mind

I share a heart with you
along the quiet,
secluded path
day to night.

Kind one,
didn't you sense love
hidden within the underbrush
of desire?
Didn't you guide
the kiss's bud
to blossom on my bitten, blood-stained lips?

Kind one,
how startled I felt
to stare at those gravestones
while pressing you against my body
and to remember suddenly a destitute father

نازنینا،
صوت سازت
خاطری در دوردست ذهن
می‌کارد

با تو دارم دل
در مسیری
خلوت و خاموش
شب تا روز.

نازنینا،
عشق را در بوته‌ی شهوت
نبوییدی؟
بوسه را در درد خون‌آلود لب
چون غنچه
نشگفتی؟

نازنینا،
چه مرور قبر در آغوش تو خوش بود
و نگاه ناتوان آن پدر

Green
  –the growth of my solitude
  in your heart

Yellow
  –your cheeks greeting
  the sun at dawn

Orange
  –your belly warm
  as a fire during
  a stormy night
  and a resting place
  for my hands

and Red
  –when your lips seek mine,
  and kiss wildly
  like a bee drunk
  from a daisy's pollen.

❊ ❊ ❊

Music resonates the emergency of love
in our dance of celebration,
and your legs that bear the urgency of life
remain the hiding place
for my return.

سبز،
ـرشد تنهایی من
در دل تو.

زرد،
ـگونه‌هایت هر صبح
در سلام خورشید.

نارنجی،
ـشکمت گرم
(همچو آتشدانی در شبی طوفانی)
استراحت‌گاهی
که بر آن دست من می‌آرامد

و به رنگ قرمز،
ـوقتی لب تو
وحشیانه به شکار لب من می‌آید
مثل زنبوری مست
به شکار گل مروارید،

❊ ❊ ❊

طنین ممتد موسیقی
ضرورت عشق را
تکرار می‌کند
در رقص شادی ما
و دو پایت
که جایگاه نیاز
پناهگاه من است
در برگشت.

with blossoming
delight
and birth.

Let me breathe your beauty
so that I
inspired by you
can ignite these people
with love,

and these lovers
would radiate
your light
that shimmers like a silken camisole,
the prism of dusk,
or a forest at dawn:

Purple
–your breasts bruised by my caresses.

Indigo
–my teeth marks
on your skin

Blue
–your watery eyes
(in my memory)
at the moment of departure

تازگی،
سرخوشی
و
زایش را.

بگذار
تا که آبستن زیبایی تو
این جماعت را
من
شعله‌ور سازم
با آتش عشق.
و چنین عشاقی
پرتوی نور تو را می‌پاشند
ـ هم‌چنان جامه‌ی ابریشمی مواجی ـ
در بلور مغرب
یا طلوع جنگل:

بنفش،
ـ سینه‌ات سخت کبود
در کف دست نوازشگر من.

نیلی،
ـ داغ دندان من
بر پوست تو.

آبی،
ـ چشم گریان تو در
لحظه‌ی کوچ من از بستر تو
(نقش جاویدی در خاطره‌ام)

The Emergency of Love

I'm a solitary tree
grown
in a scorched desert
  –this land–
and you
a foreign hurricane.

Drench me in the cloudburst
of your fingertips.
Inside me,
    your rain creates
    a color for each lover.

Dazzling rainbow,
nestled between your breasts
like a single, drawn arrow in a warrior's bow,
    your light blazes like an artist's palette

ضرورت عشق

من درختی تنها
در کویری سوزان
ـ این خاک ـ
و تو
طوفانی بیگانه
از دیاری دور.

پر کن از رگباری
کز سرانگشت تو می‌ریزد
اندرونم را،
تا که هر قطره‌ی آن
معشوقی را تصویر کند
ـ هر یکی با رنگی.

و درخشنده کمان
خفته در قوس دو پستانت
تیر آرش را پرواز دهد،
تا بیفشاند نور
همچو لوحی از رنگ

«رقص» معانی خاص و ارتباط فرهنگی ویژه‌ای را در بر می‌گیرند که برای انتقال فرهنگی و بیانی، ساختاری دیگرگونه می‌طلبد. مثلاً در برگردان شعر «دوست نداشتن خطرناک است» بیل، عبارت "dance floor to make time new" با چنین مشکلی روبه‌روست. چرا که در آن استعاره‌ای به‌کار رفته که از پیش‌فرض‌های فرهنگیِ غالب به دور است. علاوه بر این در فارسی این عبارت تعرضی به عادت‌های اجتماعی متداول است که در آن تماس فیزیکی بین دو جنس مخالف در محافل عمومی نادر است. پس رقصیدن به محل‌های خصوصی، با شرکت جمعی خاص منتقل می‌شود. در نتیجه به اجبار این عبارت در تشخیص فرهنگیِ معاصر زبان فارسی تعبیری دیگرگونه خواهد داشت.

از سوی دیگر کنایه‌ها و اشاره‌های مکرر به اسطوره، ادبیات و مذهب که در شعر محمود موجود است، برای خواننده‌ی انگلیسی‌زبان شناخته نیست. مثلاً او در یکی از سروده‌های خود به افسانه‌ی آرش اشاره دارد. به‌طور معمول خواننده‌ی انگلیسی‌زبان، افسانه‌ی این قهرمان اسطوره‌ای ایران‌زمین را که حقارت اعمال‌شده بر کشورش را با پرتاب تیری از جان به پیروزی مردم خود بدل کرد، نمی‌شناسد.

همچنین ترجمه‌ی بعضی اشارات ادبی و مذهبی موجود نیز به‌سختی امکان‌پذیر است. مثلاً در حالی‌که بسیاری از خوانندگان غیرایرانی واژه‌ی انگلیسی "Hadith" (حدیث) را در ترجمه‌ی بیل به معنای گفته‌های پیامبر و قدیسین می‌شناسند، اما بعید است بتوانند به ارتباط پایه‌ای قطعه‌ی «لبانت/ به ظرافتی که تکامل انسانی مر ا/رقم می‌زد/ آواز آشنایی/ سر داد.» با بند آغازین شعر زیبای «آیدا در آیینه»ی شاملو پی ببرند. در فارسی، وقتی کلامی، عبارتی و یا استعاره‌ای از سخنان پیشینیان به عاریت گرفته می‌شود محتوای شعر را به فضایی گسترده‌تر می‌برد که در آن درک خواننده دیگر تنها به شعر حاضر خلاصه نشده، او را تا سرمنزل فلسفی، اخلاقی، سیاسی و اجتماعی دیگری می‌کشاند.

همچنان که در یک ضرورت واقعی، زبان پس می‌نشیند تا تن پیش رفته تماس حاصل شود، آغوش در بر بگیرد و وداع را حرکت دستی ترسیم کند، دلیل وجود این مجموعه نیز گذشتن از زبان است و رسیدن به چالش تجربه‌ای عملی. هرچند سروده‌های این دفتر گرفتار بندهای زبان نگارش هستند، امید است که ترجمه، تسلیم آن محدودیت‌ها نشده باشد.

محمود کریمی حکاک و بیل والک

تابستان ۲۰۰۹

تفاهمی نسبی رسیده، مجموعه را برای نظرسنجی به دیگر آشنایان متخصص بسپاریم.

ضرورت عشق تجربه‌ای است که در آن دو دوستِ نزدیک، صمیمانه‌ترین احساسات خود را ورای فرهنگ و زبانی خاص، و بدون توضیح در زیرنویس مبادله می‌کنند. چنین تلاشی البته تا حدی خیال‌پردازی است و خوش‌بینی، چرا که شاعر مجبور می‌شود در گریز از مضامین و مفاهیم غیرقابل‌ترجمه با صدای دیگری سخن بگوید و با کلمات او بنویسد. زمانی که ترجمه، به‌ویژه ترجمه‌ی شعر، نه از زبانی به زبان نزدیک به آن، بلکه میان دو زبان از دو دنیای دور از هم صورت می‌گیرد، گاه کلمات به صورت معما درآمده معنی از یک زبانِ به زبان دیگر کش می‌آید و مضمون شکل تازه به خود می‌گیرد. در نتیجه موانع و محدودیت‌های موجود در زبان هدفِ ترجمه گیج‌کننده می‌شود و پیچیده.

قرار نیست ترجمه ارائه‌ی نهایی انتقال شعر باشد از زبانی به زبان دیگر، بلکه، دست‌کم برای ما، ترجمه تلاشی است در بنای ساختاری چندجانبه (و در نهایت همه‌جانبه) بر پایه‌ی نوشته‌ای خاص در زبانی دیگر. در این راه عادت‌های اجتماعی نیز دلیلی دیگر بر تفاوت‌های مفهومی و نگارشی است. شاید یکی از بزرگ‌ترین سدهای موجود در راه ترجمه‌ی این شعرها همین بوده است. در انگلیسی شاعر شعر را می‌نویسد و خواننده آن را می‌خواند. در حالی‌که در فارسی شاعر شعر می‌گوید و شنونده می‌شنود. برای ایرانیان شعر یک پدیده‌ی اجتماعی است که معمولاً در جمع به کار گرفته می‌شود. حتی در غیاب شخص شاعر نیز غالباً کسی شعر او را می‌خواند، و دیگران به آن گوش می‌دهند. شنونده گاه در صورت آشنایی قبلی با شعر بخش‌هایی از آن را زمزمه می‌کند. شعر در حوزه‌ی فرهنگ فارسی حالت یک گفت‌وشنود اجتماعی را دارد. گفت‌وشنودی که فقط در خواننده و شنونده خلاصه نمی‌شود، بلکه دیگران نیز از آن بهره می‌برند. شعر تا آن درجه با روان اجتماعی درگیر می‌شود که گاه مصرع و یا مضمونی از آن به صورت گویش درآمده دهان به دهان می‌چرخد. در انگلیسی اما معمولاً شاعر به انتشار سروده‌اش در مجله و یا کتاب راضی است. نوشته‌ای که دوستداران شعرش آن را در خلوت خویش مطالعه می‌کنند و به لذتی فردی قانع‌اند. البته مواردی نیز وجود دارد که از شاعر برای خواندن شعرش دعوت می‌شود اما حتی در چنین مواردی نیز کمتر اتفاق می‌افتد که تبادلی فعال و دوسویه بین خواننده و شنونده پیش آید.

کار پیوسته برای برگردان سروده‌های این مجموعه، پلی شد که از فراز تعصب‌های فرهنگی، قالب‌سازی‌های همه‌پسند، و تبعیض‌های خودخواهانه گذشته، کلام را از زبانی به زبان دیگر منتقل می‌کند. در نگرشی این‌گونه حتی کلماتی ساده چون «شراب» و

پیش‌گفتار

نطفه‌ی **ضرورت عشق** در سال ۲۰۰۵ شکل گرفت. ما برای خوانش غزل‌هایی از حافظ که به‌تازگی ترجمه کرده بودیم به جنوب کالیفرنیا دعوت شدیم. در راهِ بازگشت، به درخواست دوست مهماندارمان، محمود قطعه‌ای از یکی از اشعار خود را خواند. بیل خواست شعر محمود برایش ترجمه شود. کوشش برای برگرداندن فی‌البداهه، حتی به صورت تحت‌الفظی، با اشکال در انتقال برخی مفاهیم در زبان انگلیسی مواجه شد. سؤال بیل که آیا ترجمه‌ی شعر او نیز در فارسی به چنین مشکلی برخواهد خورد، ما را بر آن داشت که تلاشی مشترک را برای ترجمه‌ی اشعار یکدیگر در برنامه‌های خود بگنجانیم. در سه سالی که در پی آمد، هرگاه به دیدار هم می‌رفتیم، به خواندن، بررسی و موشکافی سروده‌های یکدیگر نیز می‌نشستیم.

این همکاری به تجربه‌ای دیگرگون با آن‌چه در کار برگردان حافظ به‌دست آورده بودیم، انجامید. این‌بار به‌جای این‌که تعبیر متنی «نامکشوف» و «رسوخ‌ناپذیر» در دستور کار قرار بگیرد، هر یک از ما می‌توانست دقیقاً معنی و هدف استفاده از اصطلاحات و عبارات، کنایه‌های ویژه و مشکل‌ساز، واژه‌های روزمره و ترکیب‌های نامعمول را توضیح داده، با کمک هم در جست‌وجوی مترادفی رسا در زبان هدف برآییم. اما، با وجود حضور شخص گوینده و وسواس و دقت در درک منظور کلام، در پاره‌ای موارد، کلام همچنان گنگ و نامفهوم باقی ماند. بر خلاف انتظار، این تجربه نیز سخت و پیچیده بود. لذا ترجمه‌ی هر یک از اشعار این مجموعه پنج تا ده بار بازنگری و بازنویسی شد تا به

مستقیم با نبض اجتماعی حاضر، هم‌زمان معنوی، مذهبی و صمیمی است. او از چیدن تصاویر گونه‌گون در کنار هم لذت می‌برد. در خطوط زیرین شکنندگیِ رابطه با تـضادِ استعاره هم‌آغوشی و خاطره‌ی مرگ بیان می‌شود.

نازنینا
چه مرور قبر در آغوش تو خوش بود
و نگاه ناتوان آن پدر
آن خوب خفته
زیر گِل باران زمین سرد.

بیل اما خود را متأثر از چندین شاعر معاصر می‌داند که از آن جمله‌اند چارلز هنری فورد، فلیپ لمانیا، مایکل مک‌کلر، لئونارد کوهن، کیت رکستون، و الن لینزبرگ. اشعار او غالباً تصاویر خود را در خواب و کابوس می‌جویند.

در میان حلولِ گه‌گاهی
بود و نبودِ تو

دری
بر سطح آب شناور است
بر آن، ما
پیچیده در آغوش هم
خوابیده‌ایم
چون برکوه یخی غوطه‌ور
و آب هر لحظه گسترده‌تر می‌شود
و خاک
دورتر.

در اشعار هر دو دوست می‌توان تأثیر شاعران صـوفی و هـنرمندان سـورئالیست را مشاهده کرد. در جریان ترجمه‌ی این اشعار، تلاش بیل در سورئال کردن اشعار محمود است و کوشش محمود در ترسیم صوفیانه‌ی تصاویر بیل.

خسرو شمیرانی
مونترال
تابستان ۲۰۰۹

می‌رفت و محمود نیز به جلسات شعرخوانی بیل در نیوجرسی و نیویورک.

علاقه‌ی مشترک بیل و محمود به ادبیات کهن ایران، به‌خصوص اشعار حافظ و مولانا نیز در ادامه‌ی این دوستی نقشی به‌سزا داشت. در اولین شب آشنایی، پس از معرفی‌های معمول، صحبت حافظ به میان آمد. آن شب محمود تفائلی به دیوان خواجه‌ی شیراز زد و تمام شب به تلاش او در انتقال مفهوم این غزل گذشت. در دیدارهای پس از آن شب نیز همواره بحث حافظ بود و غزل‌های بی‌مانند او.

ایده‌ی ترجمه‌ای مشترک از حافظ اما، اولین بار در سال ۲۰۰۰ به میان آمد. محمود که تازه از سفر هفت ساله‌اش به ایران بازگشته بود (۱۹۹۲_۱۹۹۹) در شهر نیویورک، نمایشی بر اساس مثنوی مولوی به‌روی صحنه برد. بیل برای دیدن این نمایش به نیویورک رفت. دو رفیق مثل همیشه پس از اجرا به صحبتی طولانی درباره‌ی متن و نحوه‌ی اجرا نشستند. آن شب موضوع ترجمه‌ی تازه‌ای از اشعار شعرای کلاسیک ایران پیش آمد. در پایان با برگردان چند غزل حافظ موافقت شد. اما تدریس محمود در تگزاس این کار را به تأخیر انداخت، تا سال ۲۰۰۲ که او پیشنهاد تدریس در دانشگاه سی‌انا را پذیرفت و به ایالت نیویورک نقل‌مکان کرد.

برای این دو، روند ترجمه‌ی حافظ به کشف ابعاد ژرف‌تری از دوستی انجامید. این همکاری که بیش از ۵ سال طول کشید، تأملی صبورانه در درک عشق، اشتیاق، زوال و آزادی را باعث شد. نتیجه‌ی این تلاش کتاب **معشوق عشق تو: ۵۱ غزل از حافظ** است که توسط "Cross-Cultural Communications" به چاپ رسیده است. میوه‌ی دیگر این همکاری، سفر بیل به ایران در سال ۲۰۰۷ بود که به همراه گروهی از "Civilian Diplomats" با حمایت "Fellowship of Reconciliation"، یکی از قدیمی‌ترین و معروف‌ترین سازمان‌های غیردولتی صلح در آمریکا، انجام شد. در این سفر بیل به شیراز و دیدار مزار عشق‌آفرین حافظ رفت.

انگیزه‌ی مشترکی که محمود و بیل را به هم نزدیک می‌کند «مقام عشق» است. آن هم در دنیایی مالامال از بیگانگی و بیزاری، بیداد و ستم، ناپایداری و زوال، و حرص و آز. هم از این‌روست که نام **ضرورت عشق** برای این دفترچه انتخاب شده است. ***ضرورت عشق*** تلاشی است در ایجاد پلی از کلام شاعر به ذهن خواننده. بی‌تابی عشق، به شعر بیل توان طی فراز این پل را می‌دهد و لمس بی‌پرده‌ی عشق، شعر محمود را در سراشیب آن می‌غلطاند.

آموزگاران شعری محمود بسیارند که از آن جمله، در میان پیشینیان حافظ و مولوی و در میان معاصران فروغ و سهراب بر دیگران پیشی می‌گیرند. شعر محمود در تماسی

سرآغاز

پل والری می‌گوید: «موجوداتی که به صورت اتفاقی پا به عرصه‌ی وجود گذاشته‌اند تنها به صورت اتفاقی می‌توانند هم‌آهنگ شوند.» گرچه دوستی‌ها به‌طور اتفاقی ایجاد می‌شوند، روابطی که در طول سال‌ها شکل گرفته، شکوفا می‌شوند، ارمغان تلاش و اشتیاقی هستند که لازمه‌ی ادامه‌ی پیوند در دنیایی لبریز از الزام ناگزیر آشفتگی‌ها، دگرگونی‌ها و گسیختگی‌ها است.

بیش از ۳۰ سال است که محمود کریمی حکاک و بیل والک دوستی خود را حفظ کرده‌اند، آن هم در شرایطی که بیشتر این زمان را فرسنگ‌ها با هم فاصله داشته‌اند. آن‌ها در اواخر دهه‌ی ۷۰ زمانی که دوره‌ی فوق‌لیسانس را می‌گذراندند، در دانشگاه راتگرز ایالت نیوجرسی با هم آشنا شدند. بیل ادبیات تطبیقی می‌خواند و محمود کارگردانی تئاتر.

کتاب حاضر میوه‌ی رشد روزافزون این دوستی است و این‌که محمود و بیل همواره در شوروشوق تراوش‌های ذوقی و خلاق یکدیگر شریک بوده‌اند. بیل این ۳۰ سال را در ایالت نیوجرسی ساکن ماند در حالی که محمود در ادامه‌ی زندگی سالک‌مآبانه‌ی خویش از نیوجرسی به نیویورک، بلژیک، آلمان، انگلیس، ایران، مری‌لند و تگزاس سفر کرد. اما دو دوست همواره، با نامه، تلفن، ای‌میل و دیدارهای گاه‌گاه تماس‌شان را حفظ کردند. علاوه بر شرکت مشترک در کنفرانس‌ها و گردهم‌آیی‌های مربوط به خاورمیانه، بیل به دیدن آفرینش‌های هنری محمود در نیوجرسی، نیویورک و مری‌لند

نمی‌شناختم هم‌چنانکه دوستان آمریکاییم با شنیدن اشعار فوق‌العاده‌ی فرخزاد، سپهری، شاملو و دیگران دچار حیرت شده و تازه کشف می‌کنند که شعر فارسی با حافظ و خیام به پایان نرسیده است.

فضای پرمخاطره‌ی اجتماعی و سیاسی امروز در جهان از تنهایی‌ها و بی‌اعتمادی‌های انسان‌ها نسبت به هم حکایت می‌کند. این مخاطرات با ناآگاهی‌های فرهنگی عمیق‌تر و جبران‌ناپذیرتر می‌شوند. در این فضا، اگر امیدی به شنیدن صدای هم داشته باشیم، رسانه‌اش خلاقیت هنری انسان‌هاست. از این‌رو، پلی که محمود کریمی حکاک و بیل والک از لحظه‌های شاعرانه میان دنیاهای یکدیگر ساخته‌اند روزنی است به نور و شعری که شاه‌بیت‌اش این است: دوست نداشتن خطرناک است.

فاطمه کشاورز
دانشگاه سن‌-لویی، واشنگتن
تابستان ۲۰۰۹

در ساخت انگلیسی این شعر، بیل مفهوم خسته بودن «از ادامه‌ی شب» را که بر ذهن سنگینی می‌کند، اما بار ویژه‌ای از نومیدی در آن نیست، در برگردان شعری خود به "Because of the interminable night" ترجمه می‌کند که در واقع «به خاطر شب پایان‌نیافتنی» است. اما پیش از آن‌که خواننده‌ی دوزبانه از حس نومیدی پررنگی که به حضور شب نسبت داده شده گله‌مند شود، بیل «نوید شگفت صبح» را که به دنبال شب می‌رسد با کلماتی شاداب و بازیگر به خواننده‌ی خود مژده داده و رنگ نومیدی را از شعر می‌زداید: "When morning began with astonishing delight"

همین‌طور در شعر فوق‌العاده زیبای بیل والک «دوست نداشتن خطرناک است»: "It's Dangerous Not to Love"، کریمی حکاک برخی از لحظات شعری را با چنان ظرافتی به فضای زبانی/ فرهنگی فارسی منتقل می‌کند که حس ترجمه بودن را تقریباً به‌طور کامل از ذهن خواننده می‌زداید. در این شعر بیل سروده:

And you emerge from me
not as a photograph entrusting
its single memory to paper,
but as an ear's reminder
of what the eye can never reach

مفهوم پیچیده‌ی پدیدار شدن از درون انسانی دیگر و همچنین بی‌دوام بودن تصویر بر صفحه‌ی کاغذ می‌توانند دشواری‌های فراوان برای انتقال به زبان شاعرانه‌ی جدید خلق کنند. ترجمه‌ی زیبای محمود از توانایی شعری او و نزدیکی ذهن دو شاعر حکایت می‌کند:

و تو در من طلوع می‌کنی
نه بگونه‌ی عکسی
که یادگار لحظه‌ای خود را به کاغذی می‌سپارد
بلکه شنیدن آن‌چه را
که چشم نمی‌تواند دید.

آگاهی ایرانیان و آمریکاییان از سنت‌های شاعرانه یکدیگر بسیار اندک است. اگر نام چند شخصیت بسیار بزرگ مثل مولانا، امرسون، خیام، اشتاین بک، و نظایر آن‌ها را کنار بگذاریم، این آگاهی تقریباً به صفر می‌رسد. من قبل از ساکن شدن در آمریکا شعر سترگ شاعرانی چون بیل استافورد، بیلی کالینز، مری الیور و استنلی کونیتز را اصلاً

دیباچه

دفتر شعری که در پیش رو دارید تجربه‌ای نو در تلفیق دو روح جست‌وجوگر شاعرانه و دو زبان در هم پیچیده‌ی غنایی است. پیش از این شاعران زیادی شعرشان را به الهام از هم سروده و برای هم فرستاده‌اند یا دو شاعر که به دو زبان مختلف شعر می‌سرایند کنار هم نشسته و با تمام وجود کوشیده‌اند که صندوقچه‌ی کلمات و عبارت‌های زبان یکدیگر را با کلید اندیشه و عاطفه بگشایند و گنجینه‌های یافته را با خوانندگان‌شان قسمت کنند. **ضرورت عشق** با آنکه با این روش‌ها بیگانه نیست، اما اساساً کاری متفاوت است.

بیل والک و محمود کریمی حکاک پس از سال‌ها هم‌صحبتی و شناختی عمیق از یکدیگر تصمیم می‌گیرند که **ضرورت عشق** را بر پایه‌ی سفری شاعرانه که در کنار یکدیگر آغاز می‌کنند بسرایند. در این سفر آن‌ها گاه با هم قدم می‌زنند، گاه دنبال یکدیگر می‌دوند، گاه محو سروده‌های هم می‌شوند و گاه آن‌قدر در جهان خودشان غرق می‌شوند که به‌کلی فراموش می‌کنند که هم‌سفری در کنارشان است.

یکی از زیبایی‌های این کار مشترک در شناسایی دو شاعر از لحظه‌های شعری یکدیگر است. این آشنایی عمیق به آن‌ها مجال می‌دهد که دشواری‌ها و کم‌وکاستی‌های ترجمه را که از آن‌ها گزیری نیست در بده‌وبستان‌های شاعرانه‌شان با یکدیگر جبران کنند. یک نمونه‌ی موفق از این هم‌سفری نزدیک را می‌شود در شعر زیبای حکاک در زیر دید:

چه خسته بود خیالم
از ادامه‌ی شب
و انتظار طلوع
که صبحدم به نویدی شگفت آغازید.

فهرست

سپاسگزاری

تعدادی از شعرهای این مجموعه قبلاً در مجلات دیگر و یا به صورت کتاب به چاپ رسیده است.
برخی از شعرهای بیل والک در انتشارات زیر چاپ شده است.

Pegasus Dreaming, Crack: A Journal of Poetry, The Art Factory, Beyond Doggerel, Over the Transom, Poetry Motel, Re: Verse!, Journal of New Jersey Poets, ZXY Magazine, Alpha Beat Soup.

برخی از شعرهای محمود کریمی حکاک قبلا در دو کتاب ***سنگریزه‌های تنهایی*** و ***صخره‌های آرزو*** به چاپ رسیده است.

ما، به این وسیله از افراد زیر که با لطف فراوان قسمت‌هایی از این مجموعه را مطالعه کرده و ما را از نظریات منتقدانه‌ی خود آگاه کرده‌اند سپاسگزاریم:
دکتر فریبا رفوگران، دکتر پری اسفندیاری، دکتر فاطمه کشاورز، آقای فرزین تفضلی، آقای کیوان عسگری، دکتر ناتون لزلی[1]، دکتر ماریا بِنت[2]، دکتر فیلیپ سیوفاری[3] و دکتر رالف بلاستینگ[4].

1. Dr. Naton Leslie
2. Dr. Maria Bennett
3. Dr. Philip Cioffari
4. Dr. Ralph Blasting

«ما باید خود همان تغییری باشیم که امیدواریم در جهان ببینیم.»

مهندس گاندی

برای **باران** و **شاپرک**

و

ماریا

ضرورت عشق
دفتر شعر فارسی و انگلیسی سروده‌ی:
محمود کریمی حکاک و بیل والک
انتشارات Cross-Cultural Communications، ۲۰۱۰
www.cross-culturalcommunications.com
E-mail:cccpoetry@aol.com
چاپ اول: ایالات متحده آمریکا
طراح جلد: Steven Frim
عکس‌ها: تور «حافظ، صدای آزادی»
عکس محمود کریمی حکاک: فرح طاهری، عکس بیل والک: محمود کریمی حکاک
طراح کتاب: محمود کریمی حکاک و بیل والک
شمارگان: ۱۰۰۰ نسخه
صفحه‌آرایی: مینو حسینی

ضرورت عشق

دفتر شعر به فارسی و انگلیسی

سروده‌ی:

محمود کریمی حکاک

و

بیل والک

Cross-Cultural Communications
Merrick, New York

۲۰۱۰

آثار دیگر محمود کریمی حکاک و بیل والک

معشوق عشق تو: ۵۱ غزل از حافظ CCC Poetry, New York, USA، ۲۰۰۹

آثار دیگر بیل والک

شعر:

به بیرنگی یک انفجار The Somniloquist's Press, New Jersey, USA، ۱۹۷۷

ویرایش مجله:

کلاه رؤیا، شماره‌ی یک The Somniloquist's Press, New Jersey, USA، ۱۹۷۷

رایگان برای همه The Somniloquist's Press, New Jersey, USA، ۱۹۷۸

آثار دیگر محمود کریمی حکاک

شعر:

سنگریزه‌های تنهایی CIA Press, Wash. DC, USA، ۱۹۹۲

صخره‌های آرزو، انتشارات م. ای. ا، تهران، ایران، ۲۰۰۳

ترجمه به فارسی:

رؤیای شب نیمه‌ی تابستان، شکسپیر، انتشارات لوح سیمین، تهران، ایران، ۱۹۹۸

شیوه‌ی فنی نمایش‌نامه‌خوانی، دیوید بال، چاپ اول، انتشارات گل، تهران، ایران، ۱۹۹۵

چاپ دوم، انتشارات لوح سیمین، تهران، ایران، ۱۹۹۸

ویرایش کتاب:

فارسی پیشرفته، جلد یک، ادبیات کلاسیک فارسی، انتشارات مکتب زبان، تهران، ایران، ۱۹۷۴

فارسی پیشرفته، جلد دو، شعر مدرن فارسی، انتشارات مکتب زبان، تهران، ایران، ۱۹۷۴

فارسی پیشرفته ، جلدسه، نگاهی برادبیات معاصرایران، انتشارات مکتب زبان، تهران، ایران، ۱۹۷۵

آثار آینده محمود کریمی حکاک و بیل والک:

گزیده‌ی اشعار ایرج میرزا

طلسم‌های ایرانی، هنر عامیانه‌ی اغوا، توجه و حفاظت

ضرورت عشق